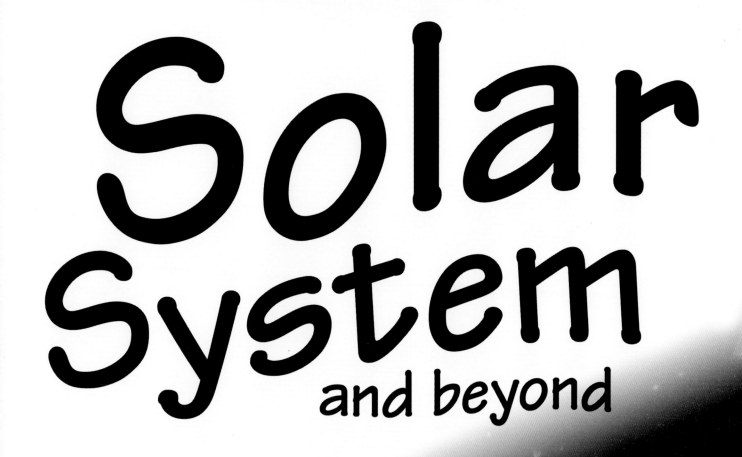

Curriculum Visions

Solar System

and beyond

Dr Brian Knapp

Glossary

ASTEROID

Any of the many small objects within the Solar System. Asteroids are rocky or metallic and are conventionally described as significant bodies with a diameter smaller than 1,000 km.

ASTEROID BELT

The collection of asteroids that orbits the Sun between the orbits of Mars and Jupiter.

ATMOSPHERE

The envelope of gases that surrounds the Earth and other bodies in the Universe.

AURORA

A region of illumination, often in the form of a wavy curtain, high in the atmosphere of a planet.

AXIS (pl. AXES)

The line around which a body spins. The Earth spins around an axis through its north and south geographic poles.

COMET

A small object, often described as being like a dirty snowball, that appears to be very bright in the night sky and has a long tail when it approaches the Sun.

CORE

The central region of a body. The core of the Earth is about 3,300 km in radius, compared with the radius of the whole Earth, which is 6,300 km.

CRATER

A deep bowl-shaped depression in the surface of a body formed by the high-speed impact of another, smaller body.

EARTH

The third planet from the Sun and the one on which we live.

FLARE

Any sudden explosion from the surface of the Sun that sends ultraviolet radiation into the chromosphere. It also sends out some particles that reach Earth and disrupt radio communications.

GALAXY

A system of stars and interstellar matter within the Universe. Galaxies may contain billions of stars.

LIGHT-YEAR

The distance travelled by light through space in one Earth year, or 63,240 astronomical units. The speed of light is the speed that light travels through a vacuum, which is 299,792 km/s.

METEOR

A streak of light (shooting star) produced by a meteoroid as it enters the Earth's atmosphere. The friction with the Earth's atmosphere causes the small body to glow (become incandescent). That is what we see as a streak of light.

MOON

The natural satellite that orbits the Earth. Other planets have large satellites, or moons, but none is relatively as large as our Moon, suggesting that it has a unique origin.

ORBIT

The path followed by one object as it tracks around another.

PLANET

Any of the large bodies that orbit the Sun.

SOLAR SYSTEM

The Sun and the bodies orbiting around it.

SPACE

Everything beyond the Earth's atmosphere.

STAR

A large ball of gases that radiates light. The star nearest the Earth is the Sun. There are enormous numbers of stars in the Universe, but few can be seen with the naked eye. Stars may occur singly, as our Sun, or in groups, of which pairs are most common.

SUN

The star that the planets of the Solar System revolve around.

SUNSPOT

A spiral of gas found on the Sun that is moving slowly upward, and that is cooler than the surrounding gas, and so looks darker.

UNIVERSE

The entirety of everything there is: the cosmos. Many space scientists prefer to use the term "cosmos," referring to the entirety of energy and matter.

VOLCANO

A mound or mountain that is formed from ash or lava.

Contents

Glossary 2

What is the Solar System? 4

Sun 6

A week in the life of the Sun 8

Mars 10

Mercury, Venus and Pluto 12

Jupiter 14

Saturn 16

Uranus and Neptune 18

Asteroids and comets 20

Beyond the Solar System 22

Index 24

Weblink: www.CurriculumVisions.com

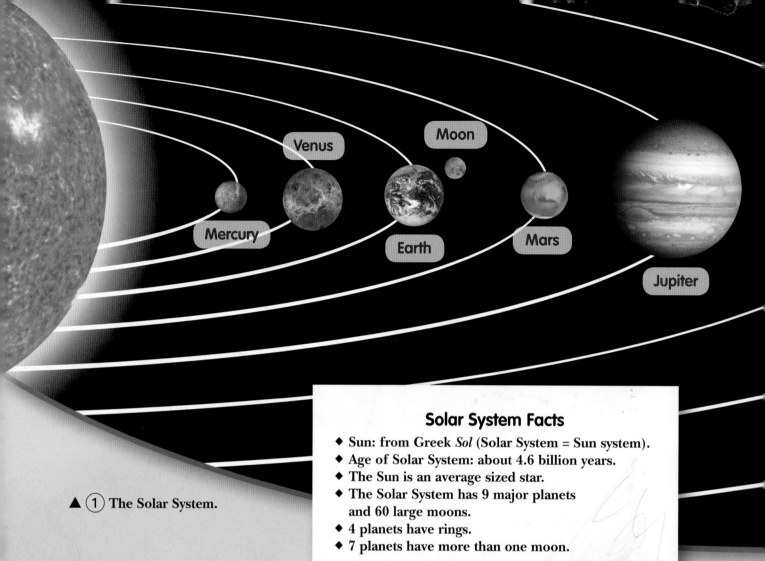

Venus

Moon

Mercury

Earth

Mars

Jupiter

▲ ① The Solar System.

What is the Solar System?

The Solar System is the Sun and all of the planets, moons and other objects that travel around it.

Look up at the night sky and you can see thousands of **STARS** twinkle across the vastness of **SPACE**. They each give us just a tiny amount of light.

At sunrise, you will see the stars fade away as the sky is lit by sunlight – the light from our star, the **SUN**.

There is no difference between the Sun and all the other stars. But our star is so close that it is far brighter than any other star we can see.

The Solar System

A Solar System is a collection of planets and smaller objects that move around a star.

The **SOLAR SYSTEM** is made up of our star, the Sun, and all of the objects captured by it, such as the planets, (picture ①) like our **EARTH**, **ASTEROIDS** and **COMETS**.

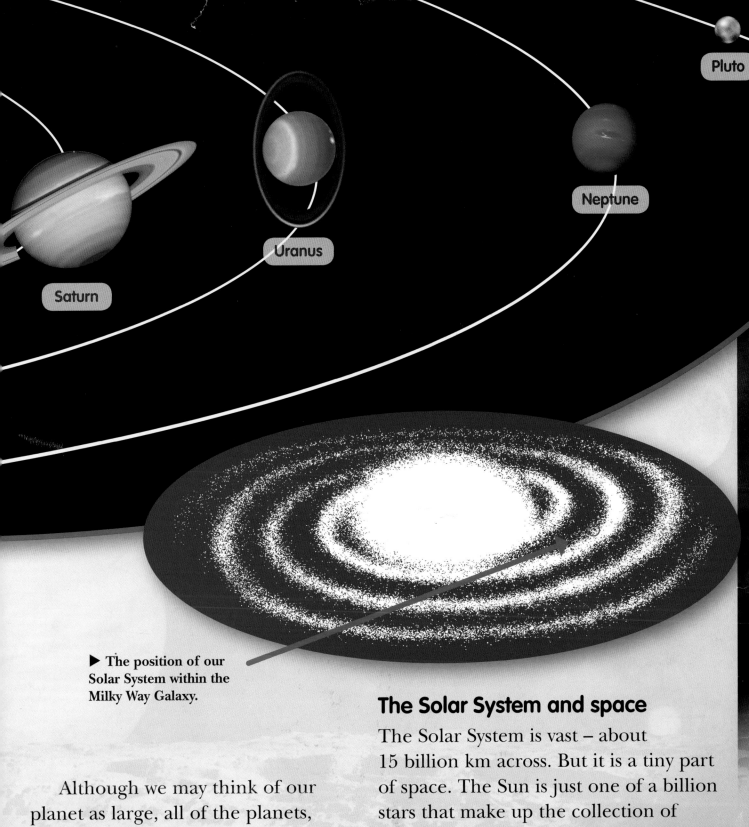

Pluto

Neptune

Uranus

Saturn

▶ The position of our
Solar System within the
Milky Way Galaxy.

Although we may think of our
planet as large, all of the planets,
asteroids and comets put together
make up just a tenth of one percent
of the Solar System. The Sun contains
99.9% of the matter in the Solar
System – all in one huge ball of
boiling gas – our Sun.

The Solar System and space

The Solar System is vast – about
15 billion km across. But it is a tiny part
of space. The Sun is just one of a billion
stars that make up the collection of
stars, or **GALAXY**, called the Milky Way
(picture ②). It takes light 8 minutes
to travel from the Sun to the Earth. It
takes light 140,000 years to travel from
one side to the other. Our Solar System
is pretty small on the scale of space.

Sun

To us the Sun is the most important thing in space, but in space terms it is a perfectly ordinary star.

The Sun is a ball of gas 1,392,000 km across (109 times the diameter of the Earth). It is so hot that it lights up the sky. It contains no liquid or solid at all.

Sun Facts

- The Sun makes up 99% of the entire mass of the Solar System.
- The Sun is a dwarf yellow star in the Milky Way galaxy.
- Radius: 700,000 km.
- Surface temperature: 6,000°C.
- Core temperature: 15 million°C.
- Mass: 330,000 times the mass of the Earth.
- Light takes 8 minutes to reach the Earth.
- Gases leaving the Sun cause the solar wind.

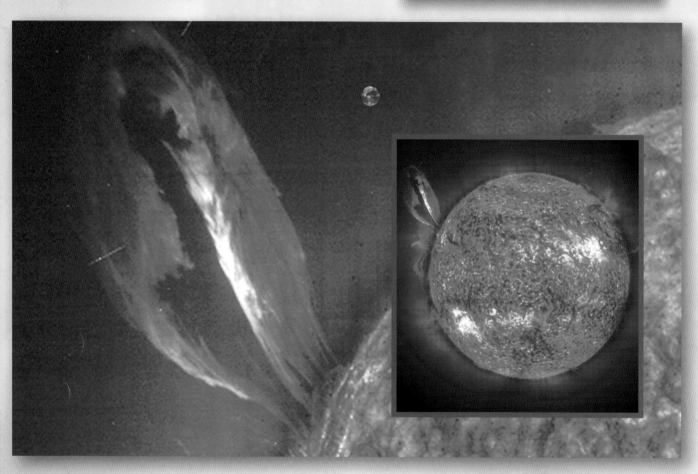

▲ ① In this picture of the Sun, you can see the surface churning over, giving light and dark patches. Beyond the edge of the Sun you can see giant curving masses of gas. These are called solar prominences. They reach hundreds of thousands of kilometres into space.

▼ ③ An eclipse of the Sun.

Silhouette of Moon

Sun

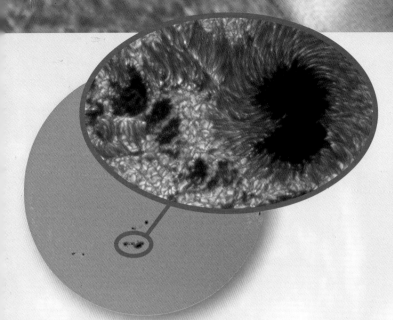

▲ ③ These dark patches in this picture of the Sun are sunspots.

and brighter, while gases going back into the Sun have cooled and so are darker (picture ①). Large areas of dark gases are called **SUNSPOTS** (picture ②).

Sometimes great fountains of material shoot through the surface of the Sun. These are called **FLARES**. A large flare can release as much energy as the rest of the Sun's surface. When they erupt, flares send great shock waves across the Solar System. We notice them by the way they interfere with radio and television signals on Earth. They also cause polar lights, called **AURORAS**.

The surface of the Sun is surrounded by the coldness of space. Here it is 'only' 6,000°C, not much different from a light bulb filament, which is why it shines with a yellow-white light. However, the centre of the Sun is at an astonishing 15 million°C!

Close up of the Sun

The Sun is so bright that we must never look at it directly or we risk damaging our eyes. But special telescopes give us close up views, and what they show is staggering.

First, they show that the surface is made from gases churning over and over. Some gases bring up heat from inside the Sun and so are hotter

Why the Sun is bright

To us the Sun is immensely bright, because we are just 150 million km from the Sun and it is 109 times bigger than our planet.

The next closest star (called Proxima Centauri) is a quarter of a million times farther away and appears 62 billion times less bright than the Sun as seen from the Earth.

Sun, Moon and eclipse

Because the Moon is so much closer to Earth, the Sun and the **MOON** as seen from the Earth appear roughly the same size. As a result, when the Moon passes in front of the Sun, the silhouette of the Moon almost exactly covers the disc of the Sun, producing a darkening of the Sun called an eclipse (picture ③).

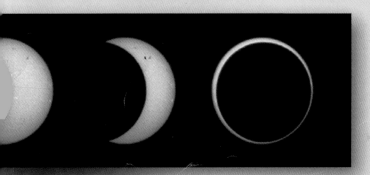

7

A week in the life of the Sun

The Sun changes all the time, sending out varying amounts of gas into space.

If you thought that the Sun was just a bright light in the sky, look at these pictures and think again. Most of us never imagine that it is constantly changing. In picture ① you can see a week in the life of the Sun.

Remember, the Sun spins on its **AXIS** once every 25 days (going from left to right as we see it on these pictures), so in a week only about a quarter of the surface comes in to view.

First, notice the light and dark blotches and see how they change from one day to the next.

▼ ① A week in the life of the changing Sun. By photographing it over time, we can show that the Sun is spinning around once every 25 days.

Look also at the lines of gas (prominences) that shoot off from the Sun's surface. You can see these where the glow of the Sun meets the blackness of space. They change from day to day.

Inside the Sun

Why does the Sun change in this way? Because it is a boiling mass of gas made of many layers. Picture ② shows you a slice through the Sun.

▶ ② This is a slice through the Sun. When we look at the Sun we can see only the layer called the photosphere. The fainter corona and prominences can only be seen during an eclipse, or with special telescopes.

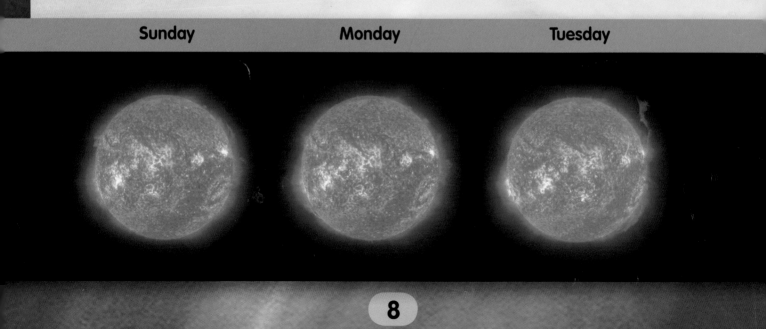

Sunday   **Monday**   **Tuesday**

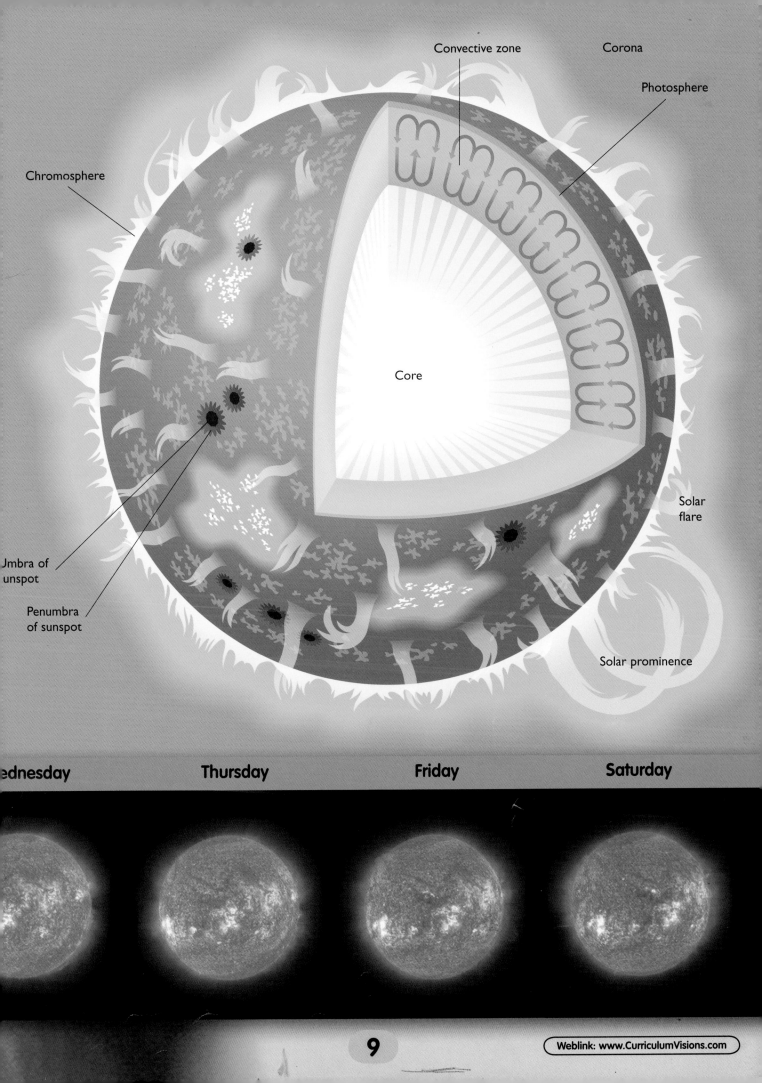

Convective zone

Corona

Photosphere

Chromosphere

Core

Solar flare

Solar prominence

Umbra of sunspot

Penumbra of sunspot

Wednesday

Thursday

Friday

Saturday

▲ ① A picture of Mars on a day when there were no dust storms. Quite often dust in the air blocks out all views of the surface.

Mars

Mars is the planet most likely to be able to support life. It has recently been investigated by Mars Rover.

Mars is the fourth planet from the Sun (picture ①). It is half the size of the Earth and only a tenth of its mass.

Mars **ORBITS** the Sun in a giant oval. This means it is sometimes as close as 207 million km from the Sun, and at other times 250 million km from the Sun. It also varies in its distance from the Earth. As a result we see Mars change in brightness and size every month.

▲ ② Giant extinct volcanoes and brown solidified lava flows are common on Mars. This is Olympus Mons, three times the height of Mount Everest and 550 km across.

The surface

Mars has no liquid water and so no oceans. Land covers the entire surface. But it is not all the same. Everywhere the surface has deep valleys and giant extinct volcanoes (picture ②).

► ③ Adirondack rock photographed by the Mars Exploration Rover 'Spirit'.

The southern part of the planet is also heavily cratered.

The surface is littered with broken rock fragments and is covered in a very thin, light brown soil (picture ③).

The atmosphere

Mars has a very thin atmosphere compared to the Earth. It is made mostly of carbon dioxide. Being further from the Sun than the Earth, it is colder all year. Temperatures typically change from −84°C just before sunrise to −33°C in early afternoon.

► ④ A global dust storm covers the planet. Compare this picture to the one on page 10.

Mars is notorious for its winds and dust storms (picture ④). Because the gravity on Mars is only a third of that on the Earth, dust is more easily picked up and it takes longer to settle. Dust can rise up and cover the entire surface of the planet.

Mercury, Venus and Pluto

These are also rocky worlds, but their surfaces are vastly different from our own. We still know little about them.

Mercury Facts

- Named after the Roman winged messenger god.
- Closest planet to the Sun.
- Radius: 2,440 km.
- Distance from Sun: 46 to 70 million km.
- Time to orbit Sun: 88 Earth days.
- One Mercury day: 59 Earth days.
- Number of moons: 0.
- Mass: one eighteenth of the mass of the Earth.

Like the Earth, these are all quite small worlds. Pluto is exceptionally small: it is even smaller than Earth's Moon.

Mercury

Mercury, about the same size as our Moon, is the closest planet to the Sun and so is always hot.

The side facing the Sun bakes each day, but its thin atmosphere means that the side away from the Sun loses heat quickly. So the surface temperature soars up to 950°C at noon and cools down to 373°C just before dawn.

Mercury is covered with **CRATERS** caused by colliding asteroids (picture ①).

▲ ① Mercury. A close up shows the cratered surface.

▼ ② The planet Venus.

Venus

Venus is the second planet from the Sun and our closest neighbour (picture ②). Venus is also remarkably similar to the Earth in size.

Venus spins in the opposite direction to the Earth so that the Sun rises in the west and sets in the east.

The surface of the planet contains giant extinct volcanoes and deep valleys (picture ③).

The atmosphere on Venus is made up almost entirely of carbon dioxide and sulphuric acid clouds, and so we would not be able to breathe it. The clouds reflect sunlight and make Venus appear very bright in the sky.

Because carbon dioxide traps heat from the Sun, the surface temperature is 1,000°C – enough to melt lead!

Pluto

We know little about Pluto. We didn't even know it had a moon (now called Charon) until 1978.

Pluto and Charon are thought to be a mixture of rock and ice.

New planets?

Recently, two new bodies just smaller than Pluto have been found. Quaoar was found in 2002 and Sedna in 2004. Perhaps there are more planets after all.

Sedna

Pluto

▼ ③ Gula Mons volcano and the impact crater Cunitz, Venus.

Jupiter Facts

- Radius: 71,500 km.
- Distance from Sun: 800,000 km.
- Time to orbit Sun: 11.8 Earth years.
- Jupiter day: 10 Earth hours.
- Surface temperature: –80°C at edge of atmosphere to 60°C and above within the atmosphere.
- Number of moons: 16. Biggest: Io, Ganymede, Europa, Callisto.
- Mass: 318 times the mass of the Earth.
- Volume: 1,500 times that of the Earth.
- Size of Great Red Spot: 26,000 km x 14,000 km.

▼ ① Jupiter, showing the Great Red Spot.

Jupiter

Jupiter, the red giant planet of the Solar System, and by far the largest planet, is a ball of cold gas.

The biggest of the planets – Jupiter, Saturn (page 16), Uranus and Neptune (page 18) – are all made of gases similar to the Sun.

Jupiter is by far the largest. It is 1,500 times bigger than the Earth. Jupiter is almost big enough to have become a star in its own right.

▼ ② An artist's impression of Jupiter's atmosphere.

◄ ③ Here Jupiter's four largest moons are shown to scale, although not in their correct positions. Io is closest to Jupiter, then comes Europa, Ganymede, and Callisto.

Although not as famed as Saturn's rings, the rings of Jupiter, and the moons included in them, are among the most spectacular of the bodies in the Solar System. Jupiter's narrow rings include 16 moons, of which four are larger than our Moon and one is bigger than the planet Mercury (picture ③)

Jupiter appears to spin incredibly fast on its **AXIS**. But what we are actually seeing are the gases of the **ATMOSPHERE** on the move. We have no means of telling what goes on near the centre.

Atmosphere

The atmosphere consists of light and dark bands of gases – called belts – that churn around the planet in opposite directions, much like gear wheels in a machine (picture ②). Set among them are some huge, long-lasting features, of which the biggest is called the Great Red Spot (picture ①).

Moons

Each moon is amazingly different, even though they are all relatively close to Jupiter (from 350,000 kilometres for Io to 1,800,000 kilometres for Callisto).

Io may only be a moon, but it is one of the most active places in the Solar System. It has many giant active **VOLCANOES**.

Saturn

Saturn is nearly the size of Jupiter and is famous for its great rings of moons and dust.

Saturn is the second largest of the planets and sixth from the Sun. It orbits the Sun at a distance of about 1.4 billion km.

If Saturn and its rings were placed between the Earth and the Moon, they would barely fit.

Saturn spins quite quickly on its axis, making a complete turn in about 10 hours, less than half an Earth day. However, it takes 29.4 Earth years to revolve around the Sun.

Saturn is nearly the same size as Jupiter, although its mass is only a third as much. As a result, Saturn would float on water.

Rings

Saturn has the most spectacular rings in the Solar System (picture ①). The disc of rings is 270,000 km across but less than 1 km thick! Each ring is made from countless tiny particles of ice and rock. They reflect the Sun's light to give spectacular colours.

▼ ① Saturn, with its many rings and moons.

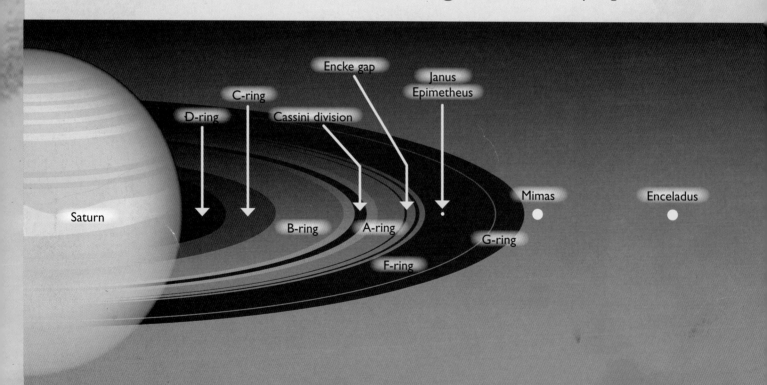

Saturn — D-ring — C-ring — Encke gap — Cassini division — B-ring — A-ring — F-ring — Janus Epimetheus — G-ring — Mimas — Enceladus

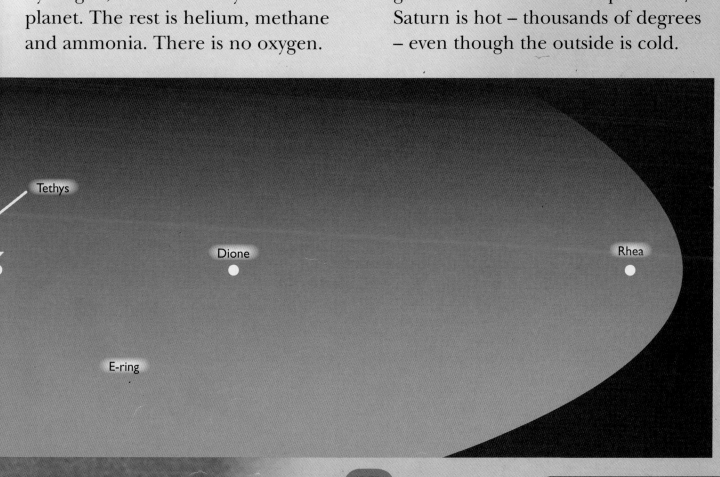

Saturn Facts

◆ Named after the Roman god Saturn, the god of agriculture.
◆ Radius: 60,000 km.
◆ Distance from Sun: 1.4 billion km.
◆ Time to orbit Sun: 29.4 Earth years.
◆ Saturn day: just under 11 Earth hours.
◆ Surface temperature: −80°C at edge of atmosphere to thousands within the atmosphere.
◆ Number of moons: 16. Biggest: Titan, Rhea, Dione and Tethys.
◆ Mass: 100 times the mass of the Earth.
◆ Volume: 766 times that of the Earth.
◆ Saturn would float on water if a large enough ocean could be found.

Atmosphere

The atmosphere is over 90% hydrogen, more than any other planet. The rest is helium, methane and ammonia. There is no oxygen.

Inside the atmosphere, the pressure increases tremendously and rises to millions of Earth's atmospheres. This squashing of the gas means that the inner part of Saturn is hot – thousands of degrees – even though the outside is cold.

Tethys

Dione

Rhea

E-ring

Uranus Facts

- Radius: 26,000 km.
- Distance from Sun: 2.9 billion km.
- Time to orbit Sun: 84 Earth years.
- Uranian day: 17 Earth hours.
- Surface temperature: –220°C.
- Number of moons: 22. Largest: Ariel, Umbriel, Titania and Oberon.
- Mass: 14.5 times the mass of the Earth.
- Volume: 64 times that of the Earth.
- Uranus has many faint rings.

Neptune and Uranus

These distant planets are both blue, almost featureless balls of cold gas.

Uranus and Neptune are much smaller than Jupiter and Saturn, each being about four times the size of the Earth. They are cold, featureless gas worlds.

Uranus

Uranus is the seventh planet from the Sun. It has 5 large moons and 10 narrow rings (picture ①).

It spins the opposite way to the Earth, taking 17 Earth hours to make a day.

However, it takes 84 Earth years to go once around the Sun. Thus, although the change between day and night is very rapid, the change from 'summer' to 'winter' takes 42 years on Uranus.

The planet appears blue (as does Neptune) because methane gas in its atmosphere soaks up the red part of sunlight and only the blue part is bounced back to us. However, most of the atmosphere is made from hydrogen and helium.

◀ ① Uranus and its rings. Background shows a close-up photograph of the rings.

The moons are mainly made of water-ice and rock. Oberon and Umbriel are cratered and so must have formed in the early days of the Solar System. Titania and Ariel are smooth and so must have formed more recently.

Neptune

Neptune is the eighth planet from the Sun and half as far again from the Sun as Uranus. Neptune is the only giant gas planet that cannot be seen without a telescope.

Day and night change quickly because each Neptunian day is just 16.1 Earth hours. But it takes 164.8 Earth years for Neptune to move once around the Sun.

Neptune's atmosphere is very cold, about −223°C. Its **CORE**, however, is probably several thousand degrees. Neptune has a number of rings and moons (picture ②).

▼ ② Neptune as seen from Triton, its largest moon.

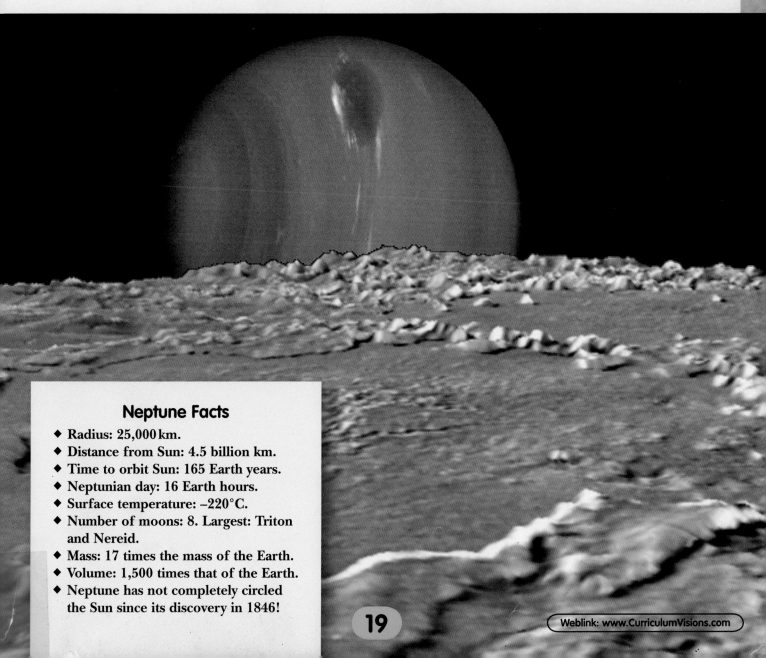

Neptune Facts

- Radius: 25,000 km.
- Distance from Sun: 4.5 billion km.
- Time to orbit Sun: 165 Earth years.
- Neptunian day: 16 Earth hours.
- Surface temperature: −220°C.
- Number of moons: 8. Largest: Triton and Nereid.
- Mass: 17 times the mass of the Earth.
- Volume: 1,500 times that of the Earth.
- Neptune has not completely circled the Sun since its discovery in 1846!

Asteroids and comets

Asteroids and comets are tiny objects that mainly circle the Sun far away from the Earth. But occasionally they can arrive on a collision course.

The Solar System is not just made of large objects, but also countless tiny rock and ice bodies such as **ASTEROIDS** and **COMETS**.

Asteroids

Asteroids, also known as minor planets, are rocky bodies much smaller than planets. They mostly travel around the Sun between Mars and Jupiter, in a region called the **ASTEROID BELT** (picture ①). They are probably parts of earlier planets that were smashed to pieces by collisions.

▼ ① **The asteroid belt lies between Mars and Jupiter. The two planets are shown here for reference. The asteroid Gaspra is shown enlarged.**

Most asteroids look like broken pieces of rock. A few are very large, the largest being nearly 1,000 km across. The vast majority, however, are tiny.

A few asteroids follow a course that takes them into the path of the Earth. As a result, collisions with small asteroids are quite common. This produces the **METEORS** that mostly burn up in the **ATMOSPHERE**. A very few crash onto the surface to give **CRATERS** (picture ②). The cratered surface of the Moon (which does not have an atmosphere) was produced by asteroid collisions.

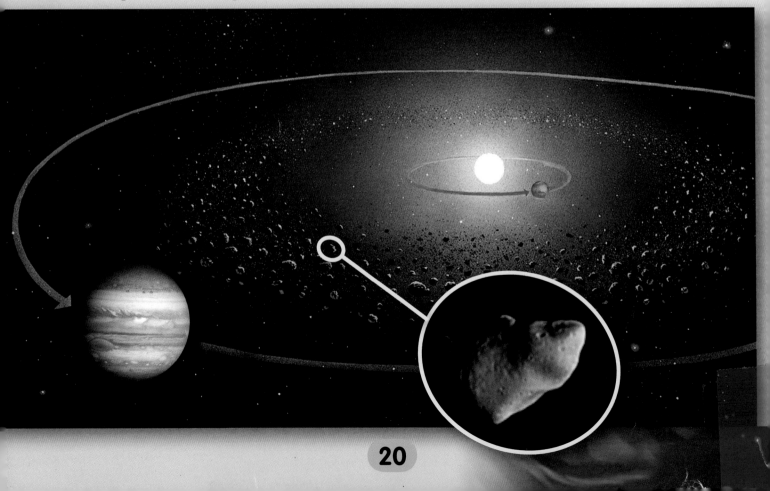

Asteroid Facts

- There are countless small asteroids, but there are just 7,000 large asteroids, of which over 5,000 have been given identification numbers as well as names.
- 30 are over 200 km across.
- Ceres is the largest at 935 km across.
- Most meteoroids are small asteroids.
- An asteroid over 1 km across may collide with the Earth on average every 1 million years.

▲ ② Meteor Crater, Arizona.

There is a very real – if rare – danger of collisions between large asteroids and the Earth.

When large asteroids do collide with the Earth, the results can be disastrous, causing great climate change and possibly wiping out many forms of life. The dinosaurs may have become extinct following a collision with an asteroid.

Comets

Comets are the most distant things in the Solar System. They mainly travel around the Sun beyond Pluto, making a 'cloud' of ice and soot bodies (picture ③). They are completely invisible to any Earth telescope.

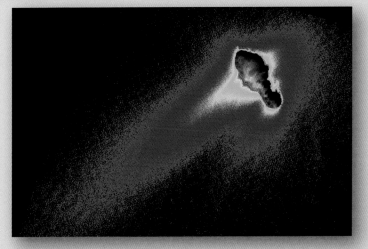

▲ ③ The ice and soot core, or nucleus, of Comet Borrelly. A cloudlike blue and purple tail of dust and gases surrounds the nucleus. The tail always points towards the Sun. Borrelly's core is about 8 km from end to end, but its tail may be 100 million km long!

Some comets get pulled from their distant orbit and then begin to travel across the Solar System, giving off a constant stream of dust and gas to make a tail that is visible even to the naked eye.

When the Earth crosses the path of one of these trails, thousands of small dust particles enter the atmosphere and burn up, creating a meteor shower.

Comet Facts

- From the Greek kometes, meaning "long-haired" which is what ancient people without telescopes thought comets looked like.
- Comets are like dirty snowballs.
- The most famous comet is Halley's Comet, which reappears about every 76 years.

Beyond the Solar System

The Solar System is part of a galaxy called the Milky Way.
The Universe contains billions of galaxies.

▲ ① The Andromeda Galaxy is 2 million light years from the Earth.

What is out there in **SPACE**? Where are the **STARS** we see twinkling at night, and how far are they from us? Can we see the whole of space, the entire **UNIVERSE**?

The Milky Way

The Sun is not a particularly special star. It has many neighbours that are both bigger and smaller. But it does not move alone in space.

It takes about 8 minutes for light from the Sun to reach the Earth. A **LIGHT-YEAR** is the distance a particle of light would travel in a year. The Sun's nearest known neighbouring star is called Proxima Centauri. It is about 4.3 light-years away. This is tiny compared even with the distance to galaxies, such as Andromeda, that we can see in the night sky (picture ①).

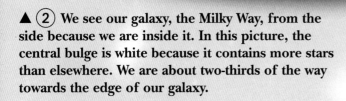

▲ ② We see our galaxy, the Milky Way, from the side because we are inside it. In this picture, the central bulge is white because it contains more stars than elsewhere. We are about two-thirds of the way towards the edge of our galaxy.

In fact, the Sun moves with 200 billion other stars in a great swirling mass called a galaxy. We call our galaxy the Milky Way.

On a clear, moonless night, you can see other stars of the Milky Way as a broad twinkling band running across the sky (picture ②).

We can never see the shape of our galaxy because we are inside it. But powerful telescopes can see other galaxies far away (picture ③), and by looking at them we know what the Milky Way must look like.

The Milky Way is about 1,000,000,000,000,000,000 km across. It would take a particle of sunlight about 100,000 years to reach from one side of the Milky Way to the other.

▲ ③ In this view of deep space we can see a yellow cloud of gas and dust (a nebula) where new stars are forming. We can also see blue white stars that have just formed.

When very large stars get old, they first explode, then collapse back on themselves, forming tiny dark stars called black holes. These suck in and destroy nearby stars. Space is a very violent place.

We have sent two space probes out of our Solar System. Since they cannot travel anywhere near the speed of light, these Voyager probes would take over 1,700,000,000 years to cross the Milky Way.

Weblink: www.CurriculumVisions.com

Index

Adirondack 11
age, of Solar System 4
Andromeda Galaxy 22
Ariel 18, 19
asteroid 2, 4, 5, 12, 20–21
asteroid belt 2, 20
atmosphere 2, 11, 12, 13, 14, 15, 17, 18, 19, 20, 21
aurora 2, 7
axis (pl. axes) 2, 8, 15, 16

Big Bang 22
black hole 23

Callisto 14, 15
carbon dioxide 11, 13
Ceres 21
Charon 13
chromosphere 9
climate change 21
comet 2, 4, 5, 20, 21
Comet Borrelly 21
convective zone 9
core 2, 6, 9, 19, 21
corona 8, 9
crater 2, 11, 12, 13, 19, 20, 21

Deimos 10
dinosaur extinction 21
Dione 17
dust storms 10, 11

Earth 2, 4, 5, 7, 16, 20, 21, 22
eclipse 6, 7, 8
Enceladus 16
Epimetheus 16
Europa 14, 15

flare 2, 7, 9

galaxy 2, 5, 22–23
Ganymede 14, 15
Gaspra 20
gravity 11
Great Red Spot 14, 15
Gula Mons 13

Halley's Comet 21

ice 13, 16, 19, 20, 21
Io 14, 15

Janus 16
Jupiter 4, 14–15, 20

lava flows 10
light-year 2, 22

Mars 4, 10–11, 20
Mars Rover 10, 11
Mercury 4, 12
meteor 2, 20, 21
meteor shower 21
Milky Way 5, 6, 22–23
Mimas 16
Moon 2, 4, 6, 7, 16, 20
moons 4, 10, 12, 13, 14, 15, 16, 17, 18, 19

nebula 23
Neptune 5, 14, 18, 19
Nereid 19

Oberon 18, 19
Olympus Mons 10
orbit 2, 10, 12, 13, 14, 16, 17, 18, 19, 21

Phobos 10
photosphere 8, 9
planet 2, 4, 5, 10–11, 12–13, 14–15, 16–17, 18–19, 20
Pluto 5, 12, 13, 21
prominence 6, 8, 9
Proxima Centauri 7, 22

Quaoar 13

Rhea 17
rings 4, 15, 16, 17, 18, 19

Saturn 5, 14, 16–17
Sedna 13
soil 11
Solar System 2, 4–5, 6, 7, 14–15, 16–17, 18–19, 20–21, 22, 23
solar wind 6
space 2, 4, 5, 6, 7, 8, 22–23
star 2, 4, 5, 6, 7, 14, 22, 23
Sun 2, 4, 5, 6–7, 8–9, 12, 13, 14, 22–23
sunspot 2, 7, 9

Tethys 17
Titan 17
Titania 18, 19
Triton 19

Umbriel 18, 19
Universe 2, 22–23
Uranus 5, 14, 18–19

valley 10, 13
Venus 4, 12–13
volcano 2, 10, 13, 15
Voyager 23

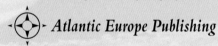

Curriculum Visions is a registered trademark of Atlantic Europe Publishing Company Ltd.

◈ Atlantic Europe Publishing

First published in 2004 by
Atlantic Europe Publishing Company Ltd

Copyright © 2004
Atlantic Europe Publishing Company Ltd

All rights reserved. No part of this publication may be reproduced, stored in a retrieval system, or transmitted in any form or by any means, electronic, mechanical, photocopying, recording or otherwise, without prior permission of the publisher.

Author
Brian Knapp, BSc, PhD

Art Director
Duncan McCrae, BSc

Senior Designer
Adele Humphries, BA, PGCE

Editors
Lisa Magloff, MA, and Gillian Gatehouse

Illustrations on behalf of Earthscape Editions
David Woodroffe and David Hardy

Designed and produced by
EARTHSCAPE EDITIONS

Printed in China by
WKT Company Ltd.

Solar System and beyond – Curriculum Visions
A CIP record for this book is available from the British Library.

Paperback ISBN 1 86214 390 0
Hardback ISBN 1 86214 391 9

Picture credits
All photographs courtesy of NASA, except the following: (c=centre t=top b=bottom l=left r=right) Earthscape Editions 5b, 9t, 16–17b, 20; Jason Ware 22.

This product is manufactured from sustainable managed forests. For every tree cut down at least one more is planted.

The Curriculum Visions web site
Details of our other products can be found at:

www.CurriculumVisions.com